BUILDING TECHNIC with BEAUTIFUL MUSIC

by Samuel Applebaum

VOLUME II

Foreword

The pieces have been selected for their musical and technical value and also because they sound very well without piano accompaniment.

By studying the text carefully, and with the teacher's help, the young student can develop a foundation for a fine left-hand technic and bow arm. This volume includes all of the basic solid bowings in the fundamental rhythms.

There are many fine Etudes by Wohlfahrt, Kayser, Sitt, etc. that are used purely for their technical value. Building Technic With Beautiful Music offers the young violin student a worthy substitute for these studies in a more melodious and enjoyable form. The pupil will derive musical pleasure while developing his technic.

After the book is completed, the student will have a set of pieces which he can play for his own pleasure, for friends, and for school programs.

THE SIGNS USED IN THIS BOOK

⊓ means down-bow. ∨ means up-bow.

A note with a dot above or below means that the martelé bowing is to be used.

A dash means that the smooth detaché bowing is to be used.

A.M. means to play above the middle of the bow.

B.M. means to play below the middle of the bow.

W.B. means whole bow (this term is approximate).

// means the bow is to be lifted. A comma (,) means to leave a slight pause, with the bow remaining on the string — usually at the end of a phrase.

p means soft. *mp* means moderately soft. *pp* means very soft.

f means loud. *mf* means moderately loud. *ff* means very loud.

Cresc. or ◁ means gradually louder.

Dim. or ▷ means gradually softer.

Rit. means gradually slower.

The measures are numbered according to phrases and should be studied by the pupil. They will be helpful in memorizing.

THE WRIST AND FINGER STROKE

1. The stroke is done entirely with the wrist and fingers. The fingers must be flexible. The curving and straightening of the fingers will be referred to as flexing the fingers.

2. Let us do this stroke slowly. Place the bow on the string about three inches from the nut, with the wrist and forearm forming a straight line. The thumb must be bent outward in the middle joint toward the hair. The little finger must be curved and placed on top of the stick quite firmly, preferably on the inner side of the bow, more toward the palm of the hand rather than at the very center of the top. Draw the bow down about two and one half inches, using only the wrist and fingers and leaving the bow on the string. Now examine the hand. The little finger will be stretched so that it will be rather straight and we might say the same about the thumb. Draw the bow back to its original position. Will the little finger be curved as it was before, and will the joint of the thumb be bent outward? If not, keep trying many times. Do not be discouraged as this is a difficult stroke and should be practiced throughout the use of this book. Spend a few minutes each day doing it on open strings.

3. In this book, lift the bow at each //. Leave a slight pause at each comma ❜ with the bow remaining on the string. This will indicate the end of a phrase. The bow, however, should remain on the string. A + over a note indicates the left-hand pizzicato. The number above the + will tell you which finger of the left hand will pluck the string.

1. The Carnival Of Venice

N. Paganini

THE SMOOTH DETACHE BOWING

1. Above the middle of the bow, starting at the middle, you are to use the forearm from the elbow down. The bow must at all times be parallel to the bridge, and should be drawn a bit nearer to the fingerboard than to the bridge. The full width of the hair is to be used, with the stick directly above the hair. The upper arm is not used, except in going from one string to another, when it is raised or lowered depending upon the string being played. The up-bow should be just as firm as the down-bow. At or near the tip, the wrist should be practically at a level with the tip of the right thumb. On the down-bow we should get the feeling that we are drawing the bow away from the body. On the up-bow there is a feeling of drawing the bow closer to the body as we approach the middle. At the middle there is a slight use of the wrist and fingers at each bow change.

2. Below the middle of the bow, we use the side of the hair with the stick tilted slightly towards the scroll of the violin. At the frog the elbow should be on the same level as the hand. At the middle, the upper and lower arm form a square with the violin, the elbow at practically the same level as the hand. Playing from the nut of the bow to the middle, use the upper arm, which moves downward and a bit backward.

2. Landler

F. Schubert

Moderately fast - above the middle (Key of B♭)

3. The Dancer

Moderately slow - below the middle (Key of G)

C. Czerney

1. When using the whole bow, start near the nut, using the side of the hair. As you approach the middle, gradually increase the bow pressure. The bow is gradually turned so that by the time you are above the middle you are using the full width of the hair. From the nut to the middle use the upper arm, which moves downward and a bit backward. At the middle, the upper arm remains quiet and the lower arm does the rest, that is, it takes the bow to the tip or as near the tip as possible. From the middle to the tip, the wrist is gradually dropped so that the bow remains parallel to the bridge.

2. When we play piano (p), we play a bit nearer to the fingerboard than to the bridge. When we play forte (f), the bow is drawn nearer to the bridge.

4. The Harp That Once Thru' Tara's Halls

Irish Air

5. Melody

R. Schumann

WE COMBINE THE DÉTACHÉ ABOVE AND BELOW THE MIDDLE

1. B. M. means below the middle of the bow. A. M. means above the middle of the bow. W. B. means whole bow. This is only approximate. You need not go all the way to the frog or tip.

2. Above the notes you will be told just exactly in what part of the bow you are to play. Remain in that part of the bow until the next indication. For example, in number 6 you are to use the whole bow for the first note in the first measure, then the two following notes are to be played above the middle of the bow. You are to use a whole bow for the fourth note of the measure and for the last two notes you are to play below the middle. The word simile means to continue in the same manner.

3. The small note that you see in the second measure means you are to place the finger on both strings. The small note is not to be sounded but the finger is to remain on the two strings throughout the length of the two lines below.

6. March

H. Purcell

7. Air

H. Purcell

WE COMBINE THE WRIST AND FINGER STROKE ABOVE AND BELOW THE MIDDLE OF THE BOW

1. Review page two and five, reading the text very carefully.

2. First practice the pieces on this page without the dynamic marks. When you are more familiar with the notes, you may apply the dynamics. In these two numbers, play forte (f) by bringing the bow nearer to the bridge. It will not be necessary to apply more bow pressure.

3. On this page the eighth notes are to be played with the wrist and finger stroke, using about two or three inches of bow.

8. German Dance

J. Haydn

9. Red River Valley

Cowboy Song

1. This stroke starts with a sharp attack and ends with a clean stop. To develop the attack, try this simple exercise for two or three minutes a day. Press the bow into the string. If the string can be moved laterally with the bite of the bow on it, and without sounding the note, you will produce the correct martelé attack.

2. We are now ready for the stroke itself. Press the bow into the string by a slight rotary motion of the forearm or a slight inward turning at the elbow joint. Release this grip and draw the bow quickly at the same time. The pressure is relaxed at the moment the bow moves. At the end of the stroke you must immediately apply pressure again. This is the rule: relax the grip at the instant the bow moves and apply pressure during the stop between the notes. The attack at the tip requires more pressure than at any other part of the bow.

3. Practice this stroke from the middle to as near the tip as possible. You may, however, start a bit below the middle. Practice it also below the middle starting at the nut.

4. The dots indicate the martelé stroke.

10. Our Life Is Work

Song Of Palestine

Moderately slow - above the middle (Key of E minor)

11. By The Pale Moonlight

J. B. Lully

Moderately slow - below the middle (Key of G)

1. Play this slowly at first, without observing the dynamic marks. We strengthen our fingers by applying effort to each finger stroke. The fingers should drop firmly and re-bound quickly from the string. The strength will come from the muscle of each individual finger and the finger action should start from the knuckle. The hand should not assist the finger in applying this effort.

2. Use only the very tips of the fingers. The first and second fingers will be well-rounded. Watch the first joint of the third finger. Do not allow it to bend inward. For the slow practicing, lift the fingers rather high and always in a curved shape. Make a daily special study of this number. Increase the speed gradually. Each note must be clearly heard and the groups of four evenly played. If they are not, it is best to reduce the speed. Add the dynamic marks when you are fairly well acquainted with the notes.

12. Menuet

J. S. Bach

In moderate time - gracefully (Key of D)

1. Review the text on page 7. Bear in mind that the grip on the string takes place before the martelé begins. The attack is a result of a release of this pressure and a quick drawing of the bow.

2. Listen carefully to the attack on the up-bow. It must be just as strong as the attack on the down-bow. The bow may be drawn rapidly at the beginning of the stroke, but should slow up towards the end. As the bow passes the middle on the up-bow, the upper arm must be lifted so that by the time the nut is reached, the elbow and the wrist are at the same level.

3. In the first measure of No. 14 we have two martelé notes in one bow. Use one-half bow for each note.

13. Saint Paul's Steeple

In moderate time - distinctly (Key of D)

English Folk Song

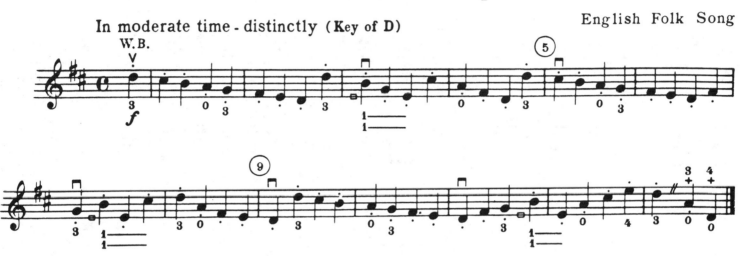

14. All Together

Moderately slow - vigorously (Key of A minor)

Slovak Folk Song

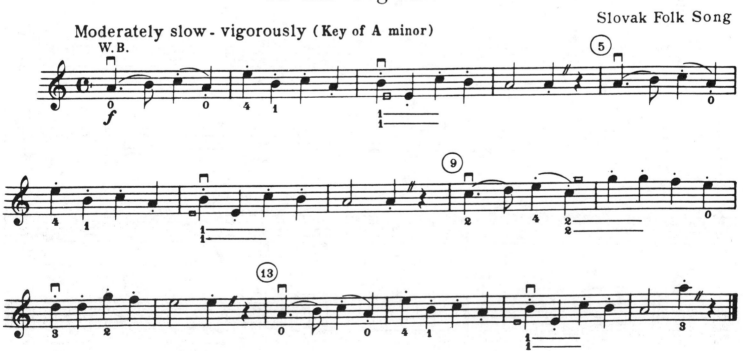

1.   The bottom number in the signature is 8. This tells us that each eighth note receives one count. The top number (6) means that there are six beats to each measure.

2.   In measure twelve of number 15 we find that there are two notes to a bow marked with dashes. You are to leave a slight pause between each note. If the notes were marked with dots instead of dashes the notes would be detached more decisively.

15. Song Of The Reaper

R. Schumann

In moderate time - smoothly (Key of C)

16. Caprice

Moderately fast - gracefully (Key of D)

N. Paganini

A variation for left-hand finger strength

First practice without the dynamic marks, then when you have mastered the notes, pay special attention to the accents. They are produced by increasing the bow pressure at the beginning of the stroke and by moving the bow a bit faster.

17. Gavotte With Variation

G. F. Handel

In moderate time - with vigor (Key of G)

Variation - distinctly

1.   Review the notes of page 7 and page 9. After you have played the last note of the first measure (No. 18) you find yourself at the tip, the bow resting on the string with the full width of the hair and the stick directly above. To play the note E, which is the first finger on the D string, dig firmly into the string for the martelé attack with a rotary motion of the forearm, which is the turning inward of the lower arm at the elbow joint. Release this pressure suddenly and draw the bow quickly until you reach the middle, then slow up the speed of the bow to make sure of two things: a, that the bow travels parallel to the bridge; b, that the upper arm rises so that at the nut the elbow and hand are at the same level.

2.   You are now at the nut, ready to play the note G, the second finger on the E string, the second note in the second measure. You cross from the D string to the E string, by slightly bending the fingers together with a rotary motion of the lower arm. Use the whole bow for this note, which carries you to the tip. In measure 17, after you play B natural (the first note of the measure), drop the whole arm to the E string to play G, the second finger on E. The notes marked with stars (*) are to be played with the martelé stroke. Since they follow eighth notes, there may not be time to produce the martelé attack. When this is the case, the attack may be left out, but you must make sure to leave a clean stop after the note has been played.

18. Sarabande

A. Corelli

19. Country Dance

Swedish Dance Tune

(We combine this stroke below and above the middle)

1. Review the notes of page 2, and play that piece over again a few times, then play the numbers on this page.

2. For the forte (f) passages, do not use more bow as you are to use only the wrist and finger stroke. Play nearer to the bridge.

20. When The Chariot Comes

Negro Spiritual

21. Turkey In The Straw

American Folk Song

Play this number above the middle of the bow, using the lower arm only. On the notes marked with stars (*) do not grip the string at the beginning of the stroke, but leave a clean stop after the note has been played.

22. Gavotte

A. Corelli

Moderately fast - with dignity (Key of D)

23. Sailors' Hornpipe

Practice this number below the middle of the bow using the détaché stroke on the eighth notes without slurs.

Song Of The Sea

Moderately fast - with spirit (Key of C)

TO DEVELOP GOOD LEFT-HAND FINGER ACTION
(Sixteenth notes)

Play the sixteenth notes distinctly. Keep strict time. Read the notes on page 8.

24. Arabesque

F. Burgmuller

In moderate time - distinctly (Key of **D** minor)

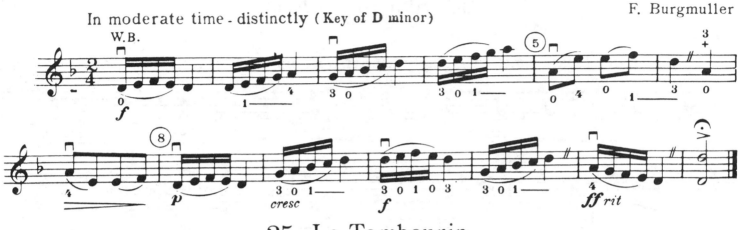

25. Le Tambourin

Here we have some interesting dynamic signs. When you are familiar with the notes, practice them carefully.

In moderate time - gracefully (Key of E minor)

J. Rameau

Some call this the Jack and Jill rhythm. If you want to make sure that you are keeping strict time count one, two, three in your mind for the dotted eighth note and four for the sixteenth note. Play the sixteenth note very distinctly.

26. Skipping Along

J. Concone

27. Change Partners

Swedish Folk Tune

Listen carefully to these two rhythms. The eighth notes are to be played evenly and must not sound like dotted eights and sixteenths.

28. Robin Hood And Little John

Old English Air

In moderate time - joyfully (Key of F)

29. Proudly We March

The small notes are grace notes. They are to be played quickly and distinctly, using very little bow. About one inch of bow for the grace notes will do.

French Folk Tune

In march time - majestically (Key of D minor)

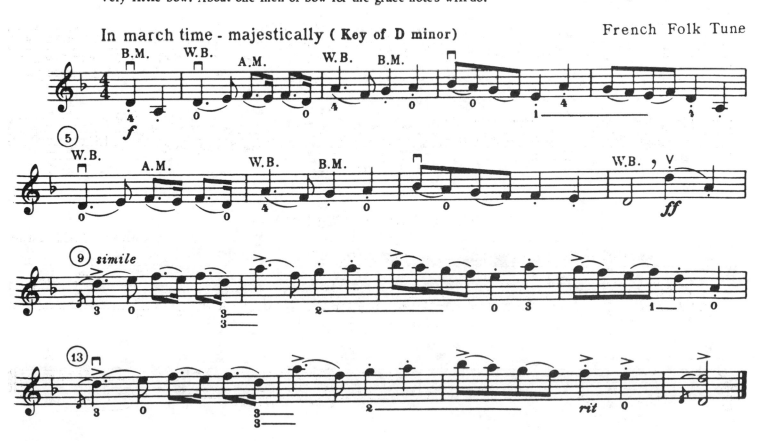

EL 1058 - 30

The eighth and two sixteenths together will receive one count. The notes that are not slurred are to be played as follows: the wrist and finger stroke for the sixteenth notes and the détaché for the eighth notes.

30. My Pony

German Folk Song

31. The Gay Whistler

Irish Folk Song

1. When the dotted eighths and sixteenths are marked with dots and are connected with a tie or slur, they are to be detached in the same bow. Leave a clean stop between the dotted eighth and the sixteenth.

2. In No. 33 listen carefully to the difference in the rhythm between the eighth notes and the dotted eighths and sixteenths.

32. Clementine

American Folk Song

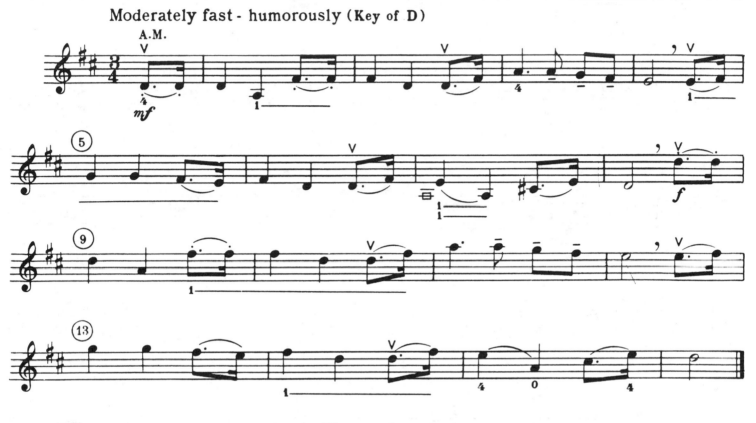

33. Toreador Song

G. Bizet

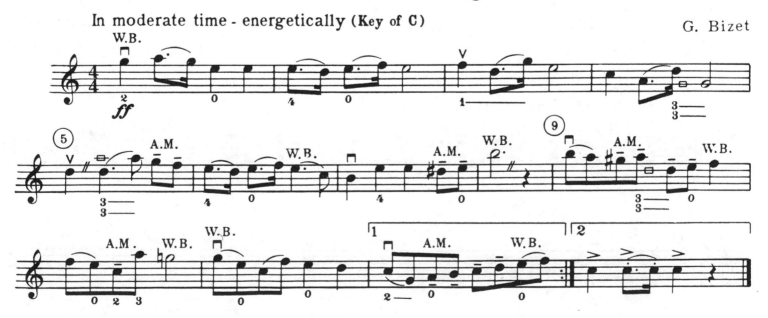

Use less bow in piano (p) passages and play a bit nearer to the finger-board. When you play forte (f) use more bow, move the bow faster, and play nearer to the bridge.

34. Mazurka

F. Chopin

Moderately fast - distinctly (Key of F)

35. Alouette

Canadian Voyageur Song

Moderately fast - gaily (Key of G)

When three eighth notes are to be played in the same time it would take to play two eighth notes, we call them triplets. The italic 3 is one way to let you know this.

36. Dance Of The Fireflies

Moderately fast - distinctly (Key of C)   H. Sitt

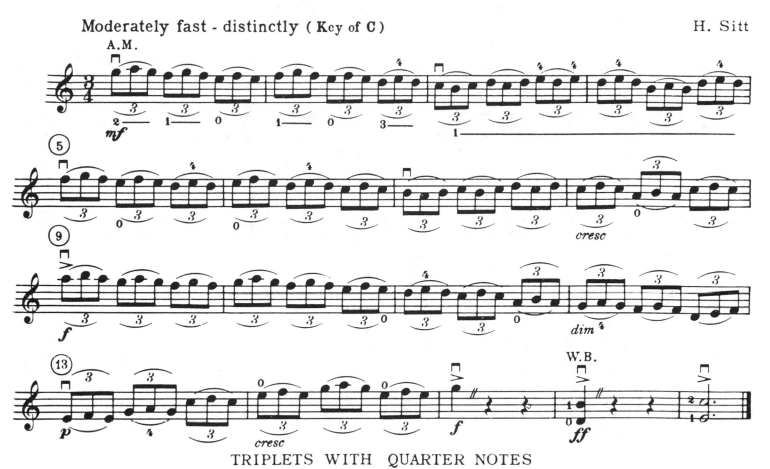

TRIPLETS WITH QUARTER NOTES

Use the détaché bowing above the middle for the triplets except in measures 11 and 12, where you are to use the wrist and finger stroke because they are to be played softly.

37. The Royal Guard

Moderately slow - majestically (Key of D)   F. Wohlfahrt

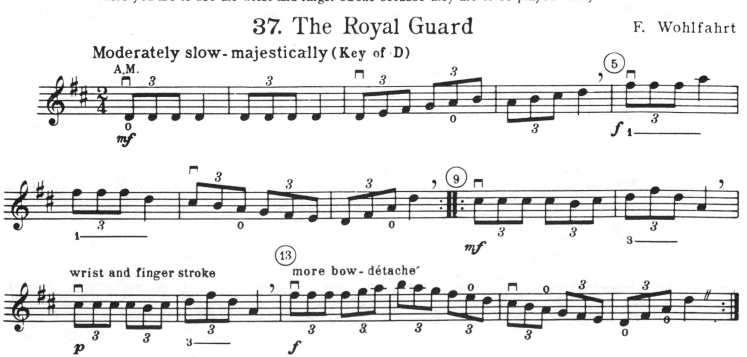

wrist and finger stroke   more bow - détaché

When playing double-stops, do not force the tone. If both strings do not sound throughout the entire length of the note, raise or lower the arm just a bit to obtain a level between the two strings. Do this instead of applying more bow pressure.

38. The Organ Grinder

F. Wohlfahrt

39. March From Riccardo

G. Handel

40. Row, Row, Row Your Boat

We now will combine triplets with other rhythms. Use the détaché stroke
of the bow for the triplets.

Round

Moderately fast-gaily (Key of D

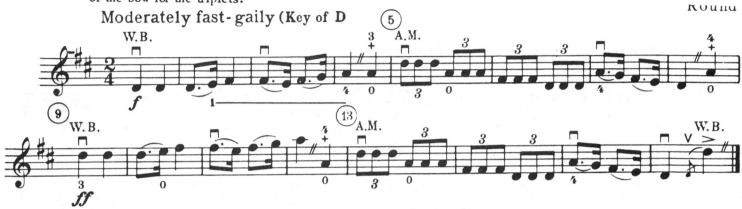

41. The Ballet Lesson

Practice this at first without the dynamic marks. Listen carefully to the different rhythms.

J. Concone

In moderate time-swinging (Key of Bb)

CHROMATICS
(To develop left-hand finger flexibility)

The finger remains on the string when going from one half-step to another. During the slide, the finger pressure must be lightened so that the finger can move quickly and with precision.

42. The Tortoise And The Hare

F. Wohlfahrt

In moderate time - gracefully (Key of C)

43. The Irish Washwoman

Irish Folk Dance

In moderate time (Key of G)

THE DÉTACHÉ WITH QUICK DOWN-BOWS

44. Paddy Whack

Irish Folk Dance

In moderate time (Key of G)

1. In No. 45 we have the slow string change which is made with the arm and a flexible wrist. In the first measure, while the note E (1st on D) is being played, the arm must move the bow gradually towards the A string, which is to be played. When you are ready to play the A string, the bow hair will be very close to it. This makes a smooth string change possible. In all playing, the bow moves towards the next string to be played, and does so in a vertical curve rather than in a straight line.

2. In No. 46 the string changes are faster, since they are in eighth notes. The string change is now made with the wrist, the arm moving at a level with both strings. If you find yourself quite a bit below the middle, a slight rotary motion of the lower arm is also used.

45. The Seven Step Dance

Norwegian Folk Dance

46. The Maypole Dance

Lithuanian Folk Song

Practice slowly at first, lifting the fingers high and always curved. Use only the finger tips.

47. The Skaters' Waltz

Moderately fast - gracefully (Key of A)

E. Waldteufel

SOME THOUGHTS ON PHRASING AND DYNAMICS

1. We have some interesting dynamics and phrasing in the first four measures. In measures two and four, the second note is to be played a bit softer than the first note. Leave a slight pause after the second note to indicate the end of that phase. This will mean that the second note will be held a bit less than its full value.

2. When we have an accent or a crescendo (cresc.) in a piano (p) passage, the volume is to be increased only a bit. We might say up to a mezzo forte (mf).

3. Notice the stars (*) above many of the notes. Read the text on page twelve.

48. A Stately Dance

W. A. Mozart

THE AUGMENTED SECOND

When we have one and one-half tones (three half steps) between two adjacent notes, we have an augmented second. In the first measure, the augmented second is between the F sharp and the E flat. Listen to these very carefully. The F sharp must be high and the E flat must be low.

49. Let Us Rejoice

Jewish Song Dance

Moderately fast - with spirit (Key of G minor)

In this number we combine some quick down-bows. In the first four measures and similiar measures, move the bow quickly for the eighth notes, but be sure to hold the half notes their full value.

50. Waltz Of The Penquins

C. Dancla

In moderate time (Key of C)

WE REVIEW ALL THE RHYTHMS IN THIS BOOK
(With two Works by Mozart)

1. In No. 51 listen carefully to the difference between the triplets and the eighth notes, as, in measure 5.

2. In No. 52 play the sixteenth notes twice as fast as the eighth notes, as for example, in measure 3. In measures 9 and 10, the quarter notes are to be held their full value. There is a tendency to shorten them.

51. At The Age Of Six

W. Mozart

In moderate time - with dignity (Key of G)

52. For Sister Marianne

W. Mozart

Moderately slow - gracefully (Key of C)

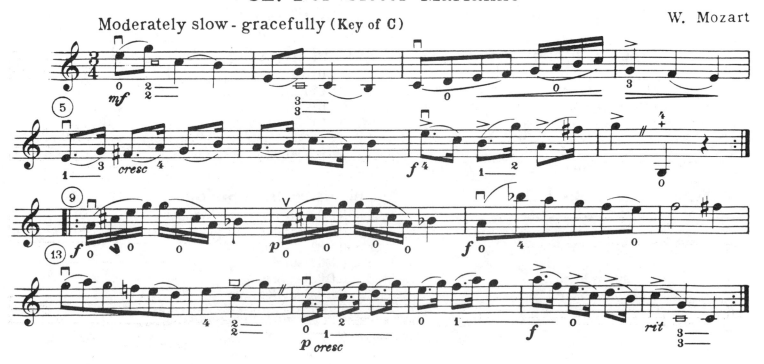

A best-seller for strings!

The String Builder Series

by Samuel Applebaum

Samuel Applebaum's STRING BUILDER series is the string class method of the BELWIN COURSE FOR STRINGS. The STRING BUILDER series is designed to have the Violin, Viola, Cello and Bass play and learn together throughout. Each instrumental book, however, can be used separately for class or individual instruction on that particular instrument.

- realistically graded material
- musical interest combined with technical value
- a world-wide best-seller in string education

Versatile and comprehensive, the STRING BUILDER series provides the quality string instruction for which the late, great educator Samuel Applebaum is famous.

String Builder, Book I
____ (EL 01542) Teacher's Manual
____ (EL 01543) Piano Acc.
____ (EL 01544) Violin
____ (EL 01545) Viola
____ (EL 01546) Cello
____ (EL 01547) Bass

String Builder, Book II
____ (EL 01548) Teacher's Manual
____ (EL 01549) Piano Acc.
____ (EL 01550) Violin
____ (EL 01551) Viola
____ (EL 01552) Cello
____ (EL 01553) Bass

String Builder, Book III
____ (EL 01554) Teacher's Manual
____ (EL 01555) Piano Acc.
____ (EL 01556) Violin
____ (EL 01557) Viola
____ (EL 01558) Cello
____ (EL 01559) Bass

3rd and 5th Position String Builder
____ (EL 01935) Teacher's Manual
____ (EL 01936) Piano Acc.
____ (EL 01937) Violin
____ (EL 01938) Viola
____ (EL 01939) Cello
____ (EL 01940) Bass

2nd and 4th Position String Builder
____ (EL 01941) Teacher's Manual
____ (EL 01942) Piano Acc.
____ (EL 01943) Violin
____ (EL 01944) Viola
____ (EL 01945) Cello
____ (EL 01946) Bass

University String Builder
____ (EL 02137) Teacher's Manual
____ (EL 02138) Piano Acc.
____ (EL 02139) Violin
____ (EL 02140) Viola
____ (EL 02141) Cello
____ (EL 02142) Bass

This music is available from your favorite music dealer.